# Pearl Drops Of Aloha

## *Oh Hawai'i My Hawai'i*

Poetry by

# John-Robert Coleman

Original Art by James Coleman

Written & Published by John-Robert Coleman
First Edition: Pearl Drops of Aloha. Copyright © 2004

2$^{nd}$ Revised Edition:
Pearl Drops of Aloha, Oh Hawai'i My Hawai'i.
Copyright © 2015

Heart Card Productions LLC. Honolulu, HI. 96830
www.heartcardproductions.com

Permission granted by James Coleman Gallery of
Original Art. www.jamescoleman.com

ISBN 13: 978-097186383-5

ISBN 10: 0-9718638-3-0

Library of Congress Control Number 2002104056

*Dedicated to my Father and Mother*

Elmer Lincoln Coleman and Stella French

# Definitions

ALOHA: A Hawaiian greeting denotes the breath of the Divine. Welcome.

PEARL DROP: liquid light, a gem, an idea.

HO'OULU: Of Hawaiian origin meaning to inspire, to grow.

HAIKU: Of Japanese origin, three-line seventeen-syllable poem.

SENRYU: A mock haiku primarily concerned with human nature, often humorous or satirical.

# Contents

# Preface

Join Keoni Lopaka

He scrolls upon golden sand

And lives his rainbow dream.

Now with you his heart smiles

Day by day across these Isles,

Prayed you be mine and

Laughing with no fear

Find not a stranger here;

But lovers of romance

At home in the dance.

O' paradise found,

You undraped my soul

Seeing of sweet simplicity

A boyhood dream

Come true.

*Aloha Spirit* by James Coleman

# Foreword

O' precious one

This little book of these Isles

Is a new love

To expand our thoughts

May you take what you need.

These treasures are of Aloha

In free verse, proverbs, slogans

Images and haiku

As viewed through these artists eyes.

In joy,

Pearl Drops of Aloha

Oh Hawai'i My Hawai'i

*Splendor of the Night by James Coleman*

# Oh Hawai'i My Hawai'i

I awoke to hear the Spirit of our land,
Aloha ke akua, aloha ke akua
Oh Hawai'i My Hawai'i
When I see you and you see me
Oh what a beautiful day this will be
As I give to you and you give to me
Aloha ke akua, Aloha ke akua
Oh Hawai'i My Hawai'i

I feel the power; I see beauty all around
Brothers and sisters healing their promised land
On sand and surf you'll want to play
See palm trees dancing, watch them gently
Sway
Catch an oceans wave and all worries drift
Away
As I think of Auntie in her hula way,
I hear oh that sweet, sweet slack-key melody
Calling to us to live in harmony,
Aloha ke akua, Aloha ke akua

Oh Hawai'i My Hawai'i
You are my friend and when I see you again
Oh what a beautiful day this will be
Like a precious pearl found in a happy dream
I awake to hear the Spirit of our land
Aloha ke akua, Aloha ke akua
Oh Hawai'i My Hawai'i

*Aloha Dreams* by *James Coleman*

# With all Splendid Wonders

With all

Splendid

Wonders

Visible

In our world

Deep within

You are

A precious

Pearl

Drop,

The

Indivisible

Ocean of

Divine ideas

# They Will Come...

No need despair

Our tourists like bananas

They come in bunches, and

From the mountains to the sea

Diamond Head to Kona Coast,

Catch the Rainbow Bridge!

Why these pearl drops now

Come from down under whisper

Sounds of tides thrashing?

O' Awaken from this

Dream

And the world will wail,

God-day! God-day!

God Day!

# On This Paper

Once breathed timber tree

Now

Offers life

To

My pen.

So let's paint

Earth so green

Oceans so blue,

Heaven so high

And fly

O' Bird of Paradise

O' fly, fly …

# May We Meet?

May we meet

At the center

Of

A laugh

In beloved joy,

Just call me

Friend…

# The Goat and the Butterfly

I have seen butterflies bounce

In her butter-brown eyes

Like feathers in a breeze

She flutters her wings

On his tingling skin,

A flirtatious one

She lives on a Rise

And comes down to earth

In her innocent splendor

Romance they did in plumeria air,

Island sounds they shared

Nectars of our God—

"But why always late,

Don't I rate?"

She cries alibis,

And he sighs goodbye...

The Goat and the Butterfly

*Mystical Napali Moon* *by James Coleman*

# The Listening Banyan

Sun shines from above
Shade soothes below
And while the oceans wave parade
Still…
I do not go astray

I stand tall as Banyan
Planted God's bloom
Trust in love's flow
Thy will my faith
The juice to grow
My limbs reach
For the invisible hand
Still…
Sun shines from above
Shade soothes below
While oceans wave parade
Still…
I do not go astray

The Listening Banyan

# Auntie's Calling

Puzzled looks I sometimes would receive
When I say, "God this is paradise, are we not in
Heaven?"
Until one day unexpectedly under Banyan Tree
Auntie honored me with my first lei
A rush of spirit came to play
Rainbow tears of joy falling on the same
As heaven above as is earth below
Everything sacred you come to know
Aloha, Ohana and I am  Home.


Mahalo nui loa

# My Business?

Simple pleasures

And it is passion

That offers you

This busi-ness!

*Bali Hai Sunset by James Coleman*

# Sea of Miracles

Do you believe as vast as the sea

Here one sees the fish from above

Life is strong for you to give

The love letters I send will never end

Do you believe when I swim in the sea of love?

Gaze at the heaven's high

Ponder the oceans deep

I see the making of no lie


To believe is a miracle

It's a day we say,

All be it jewels of the sea

Make it splendid; make it right

'Cause

To believe, to experience

Seeing is a miracle

# Cloudy Air Bubbles

Surface From

Deep sleep

Warning

My boat

Creaks

Squeaks

Repair,

Let go

Of that fear

# Sea's Mist Whirling

On tides of grace

Angel's

Windy-whipped hair

Dances Hula

# O' Tweedley-dee, Tweedley-dum

Once a delicacy savored
In a soup, "Sim-Dim-Dum"


O' Tweedley-dee, tweedley-dum
See me bob my head, gulp for air
I'll peek at you and pass you by


O' Tweedley-dee, tweedley-dum
In this Big Drink I now swim free
And you can't catch me,
I am Honu, the protected green turtle of the sea
O' Tweedley-dee, tweedley-dum

# Egg On My Face

I remain

Pondering

How

Foolish

Pride

Undresses me

# Have You Noticed?

Blue dolphins

See our child within

Beckons us

To come out and play,

Joy is their way!

# No Matter How

No matter

How irregular

My fear

To face

The mythic Madame Pele,

Lava still flows…

*Hidden Sanctuary by James Coleman*

# Waikiki Parking

AN ADVISORY:

Rent a meter maid

For time

Or

Your space is one thin ticket

To paradise lost

Auto,

Ride Da Bus…

# Pau Hana

Oh Yah…Is Oysta day!

Come out yah shell

Be as loose like pearls

Yah Brah,

We pau hana

Braddah-n-sista jus

Spreadin da'Aloha

# All Our Minds Lives

All

Our

Minds

Live, live

Under

Construction

At work

Making

Endless

Corrections

~xoxoxo~

# Hono lu lu High Riser

At International Market Place

Husband cannot stand

Standing

But still awaits his wife's call,

And

When the counter jewels glitter

Colors begin dancing in her eyes

Gazing at his wallet

With all her bottomless

Credit Card lines

Begins a tall story,

Material girl is

High Rise Maintenance!

# Soul Surfing

From within this rainbow dream

Riding on this long board

Indigo blue frosty hue now gave rebirth

Emanating a visible glee

Life again becomes grand with no end

And

As sure-footed is the way

There's nothing to fear, coast is clear

Paradise is between one's ears

Hey, listen and receive it in Divine stride—

You are being taken on a joy ride.

*Hawaiian Dreams by James Coleman*

# Rain Upon My Pillow

I do not know how many times

I rained upon my pillow

While beneath this Paradise moon

Basking in its amber glow

We've spoken many endearing words

That filled the circle of two lovers

Sharing the same ancient yearning

Embraced in each other's light

Pouring forth the sounds of our love,

My precious one,

This rain on my pillow you ask?

Is my loving you eternally…

*Paradise Memories by James Coleman*

# Ohana Villa Wanted

These tropical trades

Like palm brooms gently sweeps

Clean this petty mind

Where Aloha songs lift the heart

And

Spill rainbow tears fall on hallow ground

Seeing red slipper flowers

Trailing on rooftops

A sign

Love is the way we walk home

In gratitude …

# Night Flight Angel

Like a sea breeze

Her scent lingers

Last night's

Stand,

Solo pilot

Wings

Perfumed

She flies

Peter Pan Airways

To no-mans-land,

Between

Love and fear

Lands no man

# Be it so Ever Clear

Here, there be no

Worries

For

Out of the indelible shinning blue

And golden hue;

Beneath all our words is scrolled,


*I love you…*

# Where Pearls of Dew Drop

Meld into Manoa's mist,

Mosquito dreams red

*Island Memories* by James Coleman

# Thunder-Lust Storms

This aspiration to find a camp site

To pitch a tent, to make love

Like thunder-lust storms

For what is

Veiled

In

The heart

In our heat of passion--

The joining of two

Souls

Coming home

In

A Holy instant

# Wipe Out!

Cut by coral,

Timepiece gone

A sea

Surfing unleashes me.


Oh Malahini of Waikiki

Flip-flop, flip flop

Splash

Our waves take

Credit cards and cash

## "Give Us This Day"

"Our daily bread"

Our choice:

Have the loaf

Or

Pick at crumbs

*Terrace of Love by James Coleman*

# Perched Umbrella

Nestled here

Once the Queen's

Mansion estate

Vain peacocks roamed

# To My Brother's Keeper

You welcomed me to stay

We prayed, played and meditated

As if being three monks by the sea

And I thank God

We were housed

By

Holy Triad

Peace does prevail

# For Always

Do not say

You miss the love

For our love having wings

Is never lost

Listen, detachment dearest

Is a rest stop

To re-nourish the soul,

Know you're in my heart

# It is as Near as My Free Will

Unchain this security guard.

Hey, let's snatch the key

Of forgiveness

And free those hostages

Of

Unloving thoughts

# Imagine You...

Imagine

You as

Gift to someone

Grateful

To be the

Blessing of

One's Love

# Timberline Trees Quake

At craters' hot murmuring

Soup burping

Fire balls

Hot beds of lava find

Sizzling charcoal

Guavas,

Dare not a man-go?

# Cheeky Pigeon On My Lanai

Taunts me to share

Dumps my cup,

Pupu

And

Resident ants' line

My Kitchen wall

Dutifully tells me,

Get busy!

# Rows Upon Acres

Of Vita-C's

Did not these pineapples

Pick me?

And

Why with this breakfast morn

Does my Stately Hibiscus

Serve me its tongue?

# North Shore Weather Warning!

Snow cone flakes on

Swim wear,

Surfers delight—Shaved Ice!

*Possibilities* by James Coleman

# Meandering By the Sea

Tides ebb and flow

Winds gently whisper

Forgiving

And

Giving

Calling me free,

No limit in me…

*No Wake Zone by James Coleman*

# Beyond Appearances

O' Father Timeless

Winks its eye

Clueless and not clockwise

Tells of no begin

And no end

For one who journeys

On

Eternal elixir,

Showers perfect

Love...

# There is No Custom Fit

For slave labor,

Tuxedos, shorts

And

Sandals still

Work

# Hut ho, Hut ho!

Off to paddle

Someone else

Canoes?

Translation:

When J.O.B. means,

"Just Over Broke"

I owe, I owe

Off to work I go

Oh hut ho! Hut ho!

We the indebted,

Paddled heroes…

# Who-moo-who-moo-new

Coo-new-coo-ah-pu-ah-ah

A seven sy-la-ble-trop-i-cal Ha-wai-ian fish

# Pearl Drop

## Free Zone

This space does nothing,

Can you?

*Solitude* by *James Coleman*

Drop

By

Drop

By

Drop

By

Drop

Makes

Plenty

A puddle,

Stream

River

To the Sea

# Found Good

In search of a lost child

One can find a runaway,

A misperceived thought

Or was it a lie

Experienced

As wounded heart?

And it was told

Years later,

"Now you my child

No longer need wait

Outside the door

Of everything

Good within you,

Re-member

Who you truly are"

# Memorable Catch of the Day

On the confluence of the Mohawk River
And Oriskany Creek
I hold this memory of you.
Plucked from our green patch of lawn,
We bragged of having the best night-crawlers
In town

And upon those ponds, lakes and inlets
We did catch many 'award winning' fish.
For every fin-tailed critter we netted from the
Murky deep,

It was really that prized grin
I caught upon your face I can never release,
O' you lit up like a star
And
To me, that's who you truly are,
Hooked by a happy fisherman,

Your son

*Evening Breeze* by James Coleman

Under umbrella
Two vacant chairs sit alone,
Await companions

# I Want to Drown

I want to drown the sky

In the sea

To infuse ugliness

With beauty,

To wring a laugh

From pain


Albert Camus

# AM Glory

More than an ordinary flower

Our morning glories,

Always with sunrise

Dawning on our AM mind

Booming blue lavender trumpets,

Their reveille resounds,

"We are your sunshine

It's all truly divine

In these moments, our season

We are your sunshine"

# Delight

Out of this word play

Is hidden

Now forgiven

And given

A gift of song

I found

A rhythm

A voice

I call

My

Very

Own

# Lush Pearl

Oh these islands

With their green mountains and blue waters

Heal the past and helped to start anew.

From the waterfall of rain on my pillow

To the fragrant flower blossoms that fill the air

Came the light and joy of our radiant sun

You brought gifts of Aloha to mahalo,

Liquid Gems, living water of life…

# Smiley

On Paradise Isles

We join with unsung stars

Whom

Need no microphones

For

Breezy music rhythms sway

Gently a ti-leaf skirt;

Oh they just love what they

Do

And do what they love

Makes Aloha smile …

# Out of My Mind?

Mindful to mindless

I came to blank verse

Turning this "monkey-do" mind

Upside down

Spewing all I thought was the right words

Into reservoir of soul

That already knows better than I,

"Be still and listen,

Silence has its wisdom

Now write on, poetry man,

Write on!"

# Words Less Said

Words less said

Is another way

My mind says,

"Empty one's cup,

Da rubbish"

# Raw Lesson

I discovered though

Not by accident

There truly are no secrets,

Just laundry,

Like my underwear

Hanging as words

On the lines of these pages

Yes, I'm in my naked innocence

While waiting for my briefs to dry

I find a poet

Who by writing down the

Bones in the raw

Dislodged another of

Life's Lessons profound,

Hey! There's a bug swimming in my java!

# Arrived Yet?

You survived your birthright

To be here

Are you not certified?

In other words,

And should anyone

Question

Our natural inheritance,

Exhale

With no

Apology

# Breathe

There is no duty

of love's call.

I lay open

My precious one;

Let's set aside the Noise of

This world,

Let's breathe through our hearts

Our eternity…

Come light the candle

Let's be alone

Celebrate Us...

*Tropical Radiance* by James Coleman

# My conscience

My conscience

Like a church editor

Discerns my acts,

Either it's

Good man!

Or

Down boy!

# Snow
(first poem, sixth grade)

When snow comes down

Like a flaky sound

You know its winter

Because the leaves are down

The snow is bright

It glows in the light.

When the snow is here

It will soon disappear

And come back another year

# Congratulations!

While you are reading

This piece,

Gucci bride and groom

Blend day

Blossom fragrance

With

Deflower Night

In

Paradise

# Heart Song

What is wrong in me

Is beside the point,

This tune in my heart

Is what I am and more.

The Spirit-in-me is the good,

The right starting point

Here for you and me

Welcome you into

This heart,

Be still

Then let's sing!

# Hired Free-Hand

I stand as an instrument

Between two worlds

Receiving only glimpses,

One of the other

And other of One;

And

From this divinely guided hand

I make a stand

From one soul to another I write,

'Thank you Father for anew

Fountain pen,

Being on the same page

In the flow again—

Grateful to be your scribe,

Employed...

*Tunnel of Light by James Coleman*

## *Not Alone*

By the sea I'll walk with you

In reverie of simplicity

On rainbow color sands

Under a blanket of mist

Blessed by waves of grace two angels
Embrace.

Having loved before and choosing love again

We'll sing a tune or two of the resounding

Faint echoes of our Maker's melody.

Always the tides rise and fall upon One goal

Where a heart song is within reach

Playing upon strings of a child's happy
Dream;

Our soul's longing is a love
Song

Completing it through you and me.

# Lurching Shoreline

Monster sea wave

Weeps

Keiki's

Fallen

Sand castle dream

*Sunset Regatta by James Coleman*

# At Sunrise

Chickens cluck, cluck

While at sundown

Brings geckos

Click, lick

Luck!

*Tranquility* by James Coleman

# Grove of Bamboo

Yellow eyed,

Black crow sheriffs

Arrest their prey,

Nature's law has claws

## For Long Life

For long life,

Hold my breast

Pull my tail,

I fly Origami Crane Airways

# Kind Heart Seeds

Kind

Heart

Seeds

Planted

Spring

Blooms

And

Summer

Fall

To an abundant

Harvest

Fruits and vegetables

Always on our table,

Praise the farmer

# My Mother Rocks!

Knee deep in the shoreline sand of my dream

The tide appears to show me

It is moving, or maybe it's just an illusion?

Oh the ocean curls can wear me,

And this ancient rumbling from my interior
Core,

A remembrance I stand on hallow ground

Where I make my bed

Rest my head

Upon heavenly earth

For I am your

Mother

On the Pacific Rim

Freely giving to

You always…

# Child of Wonder

Once a child of wonder

I had grown older

My wounds seemed deeper and

Wondered,

"Where had my child gone?"

In trying to recall how to play

I discovered

My hurts had somehow gone astray

But then, there are really no disinherited parts.

To amend the past was one breath away,

To forgive myself and the past along the way

Frees my child to come out and play!

# Island Alchemy

Oyster yawns this dawn

Awakening us to see

Pearl is really you;

And taking a pearl

From an oyster bed

Is prying and slippery affair

As this pure extract

Now serves as our Isles

Virile tropical refreshment,

"Pearl Drops-On-The-Rocks"

# Indivisible are We

Indivisible

Are we

Picture perfect

Puzzle people

Our game board

One goal

Fits all

# This Moving Vision

This moving vision

Of Spirit being my left foot,

Which makes the right

Move?


A Koan

# Heaven Sent

Heaven sent

Water Falls

Upon

Rainbow riches,

One natural

Way

To be blessed

In

Paradise

*Rainbow Falls* by James Coleman

# Conch Shell

Conch shell

To my ear

Hear

This

Kahuna's

Echo)))

Gone Fishing!

# Miracles Fall

"Miracles fall like drops of healing rain

From Heaven on a dry and dusty world,

Where starved and thirsty creatures come to die

Now they have water.

Now the world is green.

And everywhere the signs of life spring up

To show that what is born can never die,

For what has life has immortality..."


A Course in Miracles

# To a Forgotten Song

To a forgotten song,

I rest my hand

Upon these strings

Of an open heart

To hear

Melody of Spirit

Strum this ode guitar,

A Beacon of light and sound

Of joy!

*Surrender to Aloha* by *James Coleman*

# Pearls of Paradise

Born of sand onto sovereign land
Pearls buried deep
Within the heart of
Oyster
The infinite sea bestows.

By freeing our outer shell
Our past illusions fade
And
Not one gift is ever lost or owned

In the corner of every living cell
Hidden in the puka of our soul
Divine treasure is found true and
To the light of Spirit all is due,

May one come to know, to
Experience,
You are a priceless pearl aglow.

*Warm Aloha* by James Coleman

# Author's Mahalo

Keoni Lopaka is my
Hawaiian name and I surf
With an open heart
Ride waves of innocent dreams
Play in unbridled places
And meet new friends.

What more is good fortune
To be free and to wonder?
To seek and find what's around our corner.

Maybe we'll find a secret hideout, tree hut
Sing a tune; build a sailboat, haiku
Write a book, and that's how
I found you.

Must go now my friend, surfs up!
Flip flop... flip-flop... flip-flop...splash...
Until we meet again, A hui ho!

*Good*

*Afternoon*

*Light*

## *Acknowledgements*

Inspired by the Spirit of Aloha I am grateful and honored to co-create this collection of poetry with James Coleman's Hawaiian tropical artistry that gave romance and birth of "Pearl Drops of Aloha, Oh Hawai'i My Hawai'i."

I am humbly thankful to Marilyn Keller for her intuitive ability. As conduit with the spirit of JOL, further sparked my life's passion for writing and poetic word play, I am truly blessed.

To Mr. Joseph Furgal, my sixth grade teacher and mentor, I honored the challenges and kind encouragement he gave to my then timid intellect. I made the "B" honor roll, and now it's snowing pearl drops in paradise.

Many mahalo go to those who have generously offered their talents and guidance: Stephen Ambush, Jud Canfield, and Scott Robinson. Terry Colbert, Carol Denego, Vickie Yasuno Kim, JC Kelly, Tania LT Hoon, Robert Sigall at HPU, Marianne Ambrose, Danny Couch, Howard Wiig, Lolane Girard and fellow author, consultant Buffie of Hawai'i.

I offer my highest regard to teachers, staff and students at Roosevelt High School, Honolulu. Without their presence both my livelihood and this self-assigned haiku homework would not have been complete, I offer extra credit.

# Pearl Drops Of Aloha

*Oh Hawai'i My Hawai'i*

Poetry by
## John-Robert Coleman

Available at:

Amazon – www.amazon.com

Barnes & Noble – www.barnesandnoble.com

Also on request at Local Bookstores

www.ingramcontent.com/pod-product-compliance
Lightning Source LLC
Chambersburg PA
CBHW061751020426
42331CB00006B/1423